Angel Hill

By the Same Author

Angel Hill

MICHAEL
LONGLEY

WAKE FOREST UNIVERSITY PRESS

First North American edition

Copyright © Michael Longley, 2017

Wake Forest University Press
Post Office Box 7333
Winston-Salem, NC 27109
wfupress.wfu.edu
wfupress@wfu.edu

ISBN 978-1-930630-81-9
Library of Congress Control Number 2017931445

Designed and typeset by
Nathan W. Moehlmann,
Goosepen Studio & Press

Publication of this book
was generously supported
by the Boyle Family Fund.

Contents

And this old gate that claps against the tree
The entrance of spring's paradise should be

—JOHN CLARE

THE MAGNIFYING GLASS

for Fleur Adcock at 80

I

You gave me a gilded magnifying glass
For scrutinising the hearts of wild flowers
(Which I did, kneeling in water-meadows).
In the handle a paper-knife's concealed
For opening occasional letters from you.
Now that we're both shortsighted, Fleur, the lens
Enlarges your dwindling classicist's script.

II

Dear Fleur, over the years we have signed off
Ornithologically: the East Finchley robins
And wrens and blue tits significant news,
My census of whooper swans and waders
From the wind and rain of Carrigskeewaun.
We've been out in the fields all our lives, heads
Down, looking on the ground for larks' nests.

INLET

for Kathleen Jamie

I have seen your face
Among the pebbles
In a Highland pool.

Seeping into grass
The sea at spring tide
Leaves bladderwrack there.

You will have noticed
A planetary rose-hip
Hanging from the sky,

A slippery plank
Bridging the inlet
And the last of the sea,

A mussel shell
Filling up with rain
As you reach the pool.

TELLING YELLOW

after Winifred Nicholson: a found poem

Yesterday I set out
To pick a yellow bunch
To place as a lamp
On my table in dull,
Rainy weather. I picked
Iceland poppies, marigolds,
Yellow iris; my bunch
Did not tell yellow. I
Added sunflowers, canary
Pansies, buttercups,
Dandelions; no yellower.
I added to my butter-
Like mass, two everlasting
Peas, magenta pink,
And all my yellows broke
Into luminosity.
Orange and gold
And primrose each
Singing its note.

COWSLIP

haiku beginning with a line of Barbara Guest

The way a cowslip bends
Recalls a cart track,
Crushed sunlight at my feet.

NOSEGAY

Let us follow Gwen John's
Night-walk down the lanes
Picking colourless flowers,
Our nosegay of shadows,

So that, come the morning,
We wake to the surprise
Of light-painted flowers,
A field in a toothglass.

INGLENOOK

for Edna O'Brien

Who call yourself 'the other Edna',
Come visit me at Carrigskeewaun
And help me count the barnacle geese
And whooper swans. Take my hand,
Balance on slippery stepping-stones
Across the channel at Thallabaun,
Walk with me along the yellow strand
Looking out for dolphins in Clew Bay
(A bitch otter may lope from the waves,
Her whiskers glittering with sea water),
Over the stile in your green wellies
Follow me to the helleborines
At Dooaghtry. Later at Corragaun
We'll make a moth-trap for tiger moths
And cinnabars and wait in darkness
For inspiring wings. I imagine
For you, dear Edna, 'the other Edna',
This inglenook in my landscape.

SEA ASTERS

I have got to know the fawn's
Salt-marsh skeleton, abstract
Vertebrae and white ribs
In a puddle jellyfish fill
At spring tide, ghost-circles
Close to the sea asters'
Purple golden-hearted
Scruffy loveliness.

PINE MARTENS

Amelia is making up her own tunes
By first light, a shrew and field-mouse
Aubade, a cradle-song for nestlings
That escape the green woodpecker,
Her improvisations a mist-net
That entangles John Campbell's ghost
Who lived here years ago and fed
The pine martens and walked depressed
Down the burnside boreen in his socks
To Lochalsh and drowned himself there,
Her notes lamentation and welcome
For punctual pine martens scratching
The kitchen window for bread and jam.

GRANDDAUGHTERS

You have buried me up to my shins
In autumn leaves. I am taking root.
My arms are turning into branches.
My head fills with chestnuts and acorns.

TRAIN

We have been travelling across Scotland
All day, from one daughter to another:
After Achnashellach comes Achnasheen,
Sheep grazing among molehills, seaweedy
Breakwaters, two stags watching us pass,
A rainbow mirrored where a heron stands.

SHEEP

Your subject matter is sheep in a field
Foraging for grass among the rushes.
Can they hear you opening the wattle byre?
They run towards you (one is black) as you
Carry an armful of hay across the snow.

SOLSTICE

Hoping for otter-encounters
I walk without grandchildren
Into the Lochalsh silence,
The puddle-lit salt-marsh,
But curlews give me away
And I concentrate instead
On the low sun as it frays
Through a tree-creeper's useful
Fan-tail (unlike the nuthatch
It can climb only upwards
In spirals, bark-mouse, crevice-
Snoozer), before I turn to face
My elongated shadow
With its walking stick, and
The cottage where grandchildren
Draw in closer to the stove
On the shortest day, above them
Bracken-rusty Angel Hill.

CORNCRAKES

I took the ferry to Inishbofin
When corncrakes were calling in couplets
And bouncing their voices off drystone walls.
I became an insomniac islander.

I never saw one, but imagine them
Skulking among nettles, in holes and chinks,
Their ratchety presence going quiet
As I approach, then disappearing.

SWALLOWS

From their precarious nest-cup
The swallows whitewash our turf-stack.
When we set fire to their excrement
They will be crossing the Sahara.

DONKEYS

I

Have the donkeys abandoned Connemara
And hobbled away on painful slippers?
We used to converse with their heavy heads
On the way to Leenane, the Famine Road.
Rosemary Garvey, blind and in her eighties,
Cared for two donkeys at Dadreen, Harriet
And Josie, patient in their bumpy field.
She had memorised the path and brought them
Carrots with the tops on, wrinkled apples.

II

Homer compares Ajax to a donkey
Hoodwinking inexperienced farm-hands
And — obstinate, immune to wallopings —
Kicking up his heels and gobbling barley
While feebly they lambast his back and fail
To budge him till he's had his bellyful.

III

Of all young animals the loveliest,
Rosemary said, especially their woolly ears.
Her coffin has become a jennet's creel.

TRILOBITE

for Bob Kennedy

Thank you for the trilobite,
Its four hundred million years
(Approximately) parcelled
With tissue paper and two
Elastic bands, carefully.
Set free by your hammer blow
From the muddy blackness
Of deep Ordovician seas,
It finds its way in sunlight
To Carrigskeewaun, eyeless
At the fireside among bleached
Bones and raven feathers.

BARNACLE GEESE

My friend the ornithologist
Fits barnacle geese with trackers
(Powered by the sun) fastening them
Between the wings with old-fashioned
Knicker-elastic that ties goose
To satellite — and to memories
Of handstands in the playground — June,
Helen, Mina (in spectacles) — skirts
Tucked into bulging bloomers —
For this Greenland odyssey
Until, alarmed by ash and steam
From Eyjafjallajökull,
Way up in the sky they hesitate.
From what Hebridean island
Do they scrutinise the plume,
Barnacle geese with girls' names,
Girls who kick up their sunny heels?

THE ORNITHOLOGIST

I

Because they cannot make their mud
And spittle nest adhere, he
Nails a board to the porch wall
And lives beside the swallows' home.

He has placed on the canopy
Above the stove a barn owl
That supervises from its case
Our shrew and field-mouse suppers.

From the wardrobe barnacle geese
Look down on his bed, two birds.
There's room enough in the glass case
For swallows to swoop and feed.

II

He has studied barnacle geese
For fifty years, netting and ringing,
Tracking in his imagination
Their return to Greenland's cliff face.

He stays with them on Inishkea
Stormbound, counting and re-counting
The generations, listening
For their messages on the wind.

This morning at Carrigskeewaun
He identifies a chiffchaff
In flight and, no more than a peep,
A sandpiper in marram grass.

At the channel I take his arm.
I don't want him to walk away.
I'll follow him to the Saltees.
We'll ring all the cormorants there.

DOROTHY MOLLOY

Remembering Dorothy Molloy
I returned to the holly bush,
My symbol for her genius,
And discovered honeysuckle
Decorating the prickly leaves.
I gazed at the convolutions
And thought about her poetry,
But then the blueness of harebells
Was all I wanted to behold —
Until a fox's white tail-tip
Flashed from among the irises
And I started to worry so
About the mallard's deep nest-well,
As Dorothy Molloy would worry.

ANOTHER PORTRAIT

I

Jeffrey Morgan has painted me again.
I left that waistcoat somewhere years ago
But I seem to be wearing it today.
The wren has settled on my hand at last —
Shh! — I hold sea pinks in the other hand.

The climate is changing behind my eyes
(A rainbow at my shoulder suggests this).
The lost burial mound has been restored.
Jeffrey Morgan represents himself
Standing out of sight in the same weather.

II

I am holding as well as sea pinks
(That wag on the draughty otters' rock
And symbolise in the artist's mind
Michael Viney counting porpoises
At Allaran Point) another flower
That turned up near the Cliffs of Moher
Interspersed with sea pinks, bloody
Cranesbill, Raymond Piper's emblem
(Though he might have preferred an orchid).

LESSON

Colin Middleton led two young painters
(Flanagan and Blackshaw) up the mountain
And made them stand on Napoleon's Nose,
Backs to the drop, heads between their legs
Taking in the city upside down, then
Straighten up — eyeball-bursting dizziness,
Different patterns of shipyard and back street.
Colin Middleton, a damask designer,
Had begun with graph-paper, little squares.

FORTY PORTRAITS

In the Falls Road's Gerard Dillon Gallery
Jeffrey Morgan's passion of fifty years
Adorns the long wall, forty portraits,
The love of his life, Patricia Craig.

Considering *A Shed in Blackheath Village*
I launch these words in that paper boat,
Inconsequential, yet emblematic
Like the kites, sky-squiggles in another.

A beauty dressed in polka dots or stripes,
Arms folded, feathers in her hat, seated
In *Night* and *Day*, she gazes into our eyes
Out of the privacy of her single room.

On the far side of the Falls Road *Conflict
Resolution Services* and *Suicide
Awareness & Support Group*, and here
One of the loveliest rooms in the world.

BOOKSHOPS

Mullan's in Royal Avenue, Erskine Mayne's
Close to the City Hall, dusty corridors,
Aisles of books, elbow room and no more,
Our first pamphlets jostling for attention,

Then first slim volumes (if nobody's looking
I'll move mine to the front. Nobody's looking).
Death of a Naturalist, Late but in Earnest,
Night-Crossing, No Continuing City —

The terrible shock of our names and titles.
Each wee bookshop has closed, a lost cathedral
With its stained-glass window that depicts
A young poet opening his book of poems.

MENU

That time I shared a lobster with Heaney
(Boston? New York?) he took the bigger claw.
At this stove I cooked beans on toast for him
And, later, for young Muldoon, scrambled eggs
(Such a serious *dim sum* connoisseur).
The poets of my youth gather round the hob.
Mahon was unimpressed by consommé:
'Proper soup has leeks and barley in it.'

RIDDLE

I flourish between pleasure and pain.
Lovers make love during my season.
One of my names says breezy branches,
Another a young man's downy chin.
The third remains a thorny problem.
Farmers stamp on my feet for fodder.
Now I'm a chimney sweep, now a broom.

SONG

The mosquito steals my blood
And leaves behind its poison.
The ingenious spider
Wraps the mosquito in silk.
The window-fluttering wren
Has its eye on the spider.
I make my contribution
To wren-song, and then I scratch.

FURROWS

That image from the boar hunt
Of how the sun picks out
Each ploughland furrow
Reminds me of lazybeds
So brought to life in Mayo
By evening sun that two
Connemara ponies appear.
Odysseus gives them names.
I comb their shaggy manes.

DREAM

I dream I am swimming
With a horse, tail and mane
Seaweedy, fetlocks
Blossoming in the depths.

CATARACT

My eyeball's frozen. I lie
At the bottom of a well.
Leaves decorate the ice.

Leaning on my eyelid Simon
Rankin breaks the surface
And reaches into my mind.

He brings implements with him,
Curious geometry,
Blades that keep fading away.

He restores the world's colours.
He has discovered them
In my own dark kaleidoscope.

NATIVITY

A starring role without any words,
The Virgin Mary wearing specs,
Maisie, little flat-chested mother
In your blue brushed-cotton robe,

The antique spongeware bowl you hold
With its abstract leafy pattern
(A Scottish fir tree) is for washing
The imaginary baby in.

In the darkness after the play
You watch December's meteors
(The Geminids) over Angel Hill
Coincide with the northern lights,

And carry home the spongeware bowl
Very carefully, still unbroken
After birth-pangs and stage-fright and
Large enough to hold the whole world.

MISTLETOE

When poets compared the golden bough
To mistletoe, had they heard about the thrush
That eats the fruit and (the seeds passing through
Undigested) wipes a sticky bum in the tree-tops
And plants the mistletoe for next Christmas —
Shit on the branches, and then pale berries?

HAZEL

Not only has the hazel you gave me
Grown as high as our bedroom window,
It now canopies a helleborine,
A wild orchid as unexpected as
The pale yellow February catkins.

KINDLING

We walk to the waterfall
And firefly memories
On the longest day, past
Elvira's weedy terrace
And the dilapidated mill,
Through brambles and goosegrass
Tangles, adder-alert, you
(Who as a child, you say,
Arranged in an egg cup
Buttercups and daisies)
Too late for orchids now
Picking angelica, cow
Parsley, scabious, wild pea,
While I, too soon for sloes
Or elderberries, gather
Winter kindling, and you
Offer me your nosegay and
Egg cup like a chalice.

IN THE MUGELLO

I

It is the nightingale's
Mugello melody
Above the parasol
That brings us together,
Old friends and new, to dine
On aubergines — perfect
Circles — and zucchini,
Heidi's speciality.
A nervy doe steps out
From the wood, then her fawn.

II

Lorenzo renovates
His antique radios,
Tightening valves and fine-
Tuning signals world-wide
From those who have dreamed here
Beneath the elbow-shaped
Roof-beams, honeymooners,
Weary farm-labourers,
The likes of me fiddling
With childhood's crystal set.

III

We are too late, my love,
For the lizard orchids
Already intertwined
In Silvano's hay-bales.
But then you discover

Survivors, harvest's soul,
Four under a hornbeam,
Other orchids as well
Decorating the verge,
Pyramids, labia-pink.

THE CHESTNUT PAN

Sunlight through chestnut leaves
Conjures at the waterfall
That jar of chestnut honey
On the kitchen table
And the griddle full of holes
For roasting chestnuts — wet
Towels around hands and shins —
Ember constellations
Beside the waterfall,
The smoky chestnut pan.

MEMORY

In the bedroom above the Post Office
(Now demolished) on the Lisburn Road
I wrote my first poem that was any good,
'Epithalamion', rhyme-words dancing
Down the page ahead of the argument,
And the closing image of king and queen
Inspired by you and me in Nassau Street
Waiting for Kennedy's loud cavalcade —
Split seconds — Kennedy, de Valera.
I phoned you and recited my new poem.
Then I dined with my mother who had baked
Cod in tomatoes, onions and breadcrumbs.
Was that the night I sat up late to hear
Clay beating Liston on the radio?

A GIFT

Selenopeltis is even older than
Cnemidopyge, writes Bob Kennedy
Who excavated it from a dingle
Owned by White Witches (lucky spells)
In the tiny Shropshire hamlet of Hope
After four hundred million summers.
He likes to think of it as feminine,
A golden-wedding gift for you (and me),
Its spines a protection as it swims
In the oceans surrounding Gondwana.

FIFTY YEARS

You have walked with me again and again
Up the stony path to Carrigskeewaun
And paused among the fairy rings to pick
Mushrooms for breakfast and for poetry.

You have pointed out, like a snail's shell
Or a curlew feather or mermaid's purse,
The right word, silences and syllables
Audible at the water's windy edge.

We have tracked otter prints to Allaran
And waited for hours on our chilly throne,
For fifty years, man and wife, voices low,
Counting oystercatchers and sanderlings.

PILLOWS

Your intelligence snoozes next to mine.
Poems accumulate between our pillows.

MONARCH

If I were inside you now
I would stay there for ages
Until the last migrating
Monarch butterfly had left.

THE RING

You give me — a golden-wedding present —
A ring made in Glasgow in 1914.
I know in my bones that it was worn
By a Tommy fighting in the trenches.
He took it off at night to read and touch
The engraving inside — GR & JG —
As we do, holding it up to the light.
We borrow their eighteen-carat love.
I like to think he survived the war.
I shall wear his ring until I die.

THE NECKLACE

Long ago I compared us to rope-makers
Twisting straw into a golden cable.
Here is a necklace marking fifty years.
The straw rope has turned into real gold.

THE BROOCH

He is talking about himself again,
Telling the truth and telling lies, Odysseus
So close to Penelope, yet so far away,
In the middle of his rigmarole, a brooch,
A golden dog grasping a dappled fawn
In his forepaws, fascinated by it
As he throttles its struggle to get free,
A clasp of such intricate craftsmanship
For fastening (in his story) the tunic
That glistens like the skin of an onion.

ENGAGEMENTS

My love letters were randier than even Guillaume
Apollinaire's to Madeleine from the sodden Front.
He writes to her about a German aeroplane
Shot down between the lines, and the aluminium
Tension-adjuster from which he has taken rings
To file down and make the right size and engrave.
He sees her nightdress riding up, her mystical rose.
A dead German's alarming tibia interrupts
His thoughts of her hymen and bloodstained calico.
(We burned all our love letters in a bedroom grate
Weeks before our wedding, incinerating lust
And unhappiness.) Guillaume's engagement rings
May have been fashioned from scrap metal only
But at least they had fallen out of the heavens.

SNOWDROPS

Inauspicious between headstones
On Angel Hill, wintry love-
Tokens for Murdo, Alistair,
Duncan, home from the trenches,
Back in Balmacara and Kyle,
Cameronians, Gordon Highlanders
Clambering on hands and knees
Up the steep path to this graveyard
The snowdrops whiten, green-
Hemmed frost-piercers, buttonhole
Or posy, Candlemas bells
For soldiers who come here on leave
And rest against rusty railings
Like out-of-breath pallbearers.

THE SONNETS

for Vanessa Davis

The soldier-poet packed into his kitbag
His spine-protector, socks, soap, latherbrush
(Though he was not then a regular shaver)
Water-bottle, field-dressing, gas-mask, a tin
Of cigarettes (a gift from Princess Mary,
The girl next door at Buckingham Palace),
Housewife, bootlaces, pull-through, paybook
And the sonnets of William Shakespeare.

He brushed off the mud at Passchendaele and,
Before going over the top, tucked away
In his breastpocket the leatherbound book
Which stopped a bullet just short of his heart
And shredded the life-saving poetry. He
Inhaled one of Princess Mary's Woodbines.

TREASURES

Among the treasures in her secret drawer
My mother preserved soiled underwear,
His medals, the strap from his wrist-watch
With dust and sweat beneath the buckle.

PAUL KLEE AT WAR

a found poem

I worked a lot, at least. Painted and drew
And ended by forgetting completely where
I was. In amazement I caught sight of
The horrible warrior's boots on my feet.

WOODBINES

You smoke two Woodbines before getting dressed
And sit up on the bed and cough and cough,
You who survived a chlorine-gas attack
(You peed on your sock to improvise a mask).

By the banked fire sit you down, old soldier,
With poker and tongs arrange the embers.
Light up another Woodbine, clear your lungs.
I'll walk to the shops and buy you gaspers.

SURVIVORS

Show us the mustard burn on your shoulder
And the shrapnel bruise on your shiny shin.
Dad, you caught one in your 'courting tackle'
And nearly lost my sister, twin and me.

BADGER

in memory of Martin McBirney, murdered 16.ix.74

Martin McBirney had read everything.
Quizmaster, he tried out questions on us,
Then he gobbled left-overs from the fridge.
From behind he was all behind, Martin.

Everyone got drunk after his funeral.
On the path to our house a badger paused.
'I can't answer any of your questions,'
I said, and the badger shuffled away.

DUSTY BLUEBELLS

in memory of Patrick Rooney, killed 7.viii.69

Patrick Rooney, aged nine, was killed
By a tracer-bullet where he slept.
Boys and girls in his class resumed
Their games soon after: *In and out go
Dusty bluebells, Bangor boat's away*

THE MOTHER'S LAMENT

after Peadar Ó Doirnín (c. 1700–1769)

When they came looking for trouble I bared my body
Hoping to appeal to them. Child of the branches,
You smiled at your mother and then at your enemies
And chuckled before they wrenched you from my arms.

When the spear pierced your chest I registered the pain
And watched my own blood spurting. Suicidal now
I struggled with them, happy to die in the skirmish
And lie with you and our friends in unmarked graves.

They tied me to a tree and forced me to witness
Your death-throes, child of the tree of my heart and lungs,
Child of my crucifixion tree, child of the branches,
And then they stuck your screams on the end of a pike.

THE TROUBLES

Think of the children
Behind the coffins.
Look sorrow in the face.
Call those thirty years
The Years of Disgrace.

THE CROSS

Where the burial mound once was
Is marked by nameless slabs, and now
A cross, an invisible Christ
Comforting the ground-level shades.

Salt water trickles from his side.
His toes are a boy's sandy toes.
A white gull perches on his arm.
He wears a crown of sea-holly.

NOVEMBER

The landscape and weather defeated me
Winded by the wind, crossing the duach
On my own but for one stranded wheatear
Far from the Sahara, that November.

We sheltered together in a grassy trench
Dug, said Joe O'Toole, during the last war
To prevent invasion: a ghost-hole
For immaterial airmen and stray birds.

A THISTLE

in memory of Bob Purdie

On our walk to the hermit's caravan
You deftly divided with your penknife
A thistle-head's miniature artichoke
And presented me with its pinhead heart.

Bob, could a hermit feast on thistle-heads?
True believer, hedgerow covenanter,
O where is your radical penknife now?
Thistledown covers your mouth and nostrils.

STORM

Wind-wounded, lopsided now
Our mighty beech has lost an arm.
Sammy the demolition man
(Who flattened the poet's house
In Ashley Avenue, its roof
Crashing into that homestead,
Then all the floors, poetry
And conversation collapsing)
Slices the sawdusty tons,
Wooden manhole-covers,
An imagined underground.
Beneath a leafy canopy
The poet, on my seventieth,
Gazed up through cathedral
Branches at constellations.
Where is he now? Together
We are counting tree-rings.

ROOM TO RHYME

in memory of Seamus Heaney

I

I blew a kiss across the stage to you
When we read our poems in Lisdoonvarna
Two weeks before you died. Arrayed in straw
The Armagh Rhymers turned up at the end.

II

In the middle of a field in Mourne country
Standing side by side, looking straight ahead
We peed against a fragment of stone wall,
St Patrick's windbreak, the rain's urinal.

III

On our pilgrimages around the North
In your muddy Volkswagen, we chanted
Great War songs: *Hush! Here comes a whizz-bang!*
We're here because we're here because we're …

IV

Smashed after *Room to Rhyme* in Cushendall
We waded through heather-stands to Fair Head
And signed our names in biro on Davy's shirt
And launched it off the cliff into the wind.

V

We drove after Bloody Sunday to join
The Newry March — road blocks, diversions —
Time enough to decide, if we were asked
At gunpoint: *And what religion are you?*

VI

When Oisin Ferran was burned to death, you
Stood helpless in the morgue and wept and wept.
Awaken from your loamy single-bed:
Kiss me on the lips in Lisdoonvarna.

THE POETS

poem beginning with a line of John Clare

Poets love nature and themselves are love.
Imagine an out-of-the-way cottage
Close to dunes, the marram grass whispering
Above technicolour snails and terns' eggs,
Intelligent choughs on the roof at dawn,
At dusk whimbrels whistling down the chimney,
And outside the kitchen window that cliff
Where ravens have nested for fifty years.

Moth-and-butterfly-wing decipherers,
Counters of Connemara ponies and swans,
Along the lazybeds at the lake's edge
They materialise out of sea-mist and
Into hawkbit haziness disappear.
One has written a lovely blackbird poem.

FATHERS

As the Professor of Pure Mathematics
At Trinity College Dublin, your father
Who was hilarious (barely audible
As a rule) would emphasize the word *pure*.
He missed out on knowing his grandchildren —
As did my father, a commercial traveller
(Or sales representative as he preferred)
A boy soldier and then an old soldier
Reluctant to talk about Passchendaele:
At night pure mathematics and bad dreams.
I try to remember your father's quips
And what my own father woke up screaming.
Their friendship's no more than a theorem
Now that both of them are great-grandfathers.

THE GYNAECOLOGIST

I

Thundery cumulus lifted from Mweelrea
When, miles away from here, Ben Murray died.
Birth was his profession, so now his ghost
Is counting cygnets on the lake, shadows
Among the tufted ducks. Swallows return
To their empty nest at the cottage door.

II

His grandsons who are also my grandsons
Watched on the high ridge above Dooaghtry
The day before he died, a bitch otter
Lollop towards Allaran and the sea.
Our grandsons could show us where on the path
The hare is most likely to hesitate.

III

Our grandsons could show us where on the path
The hare is most likely to disappear.

ANGEL HILL

Someone must be looking after the headstones.
It might be you with your easel and brushes
And your big sheets and charcoal for drawing
Snowdrop cumulus and lichen lettering.
Someone must be looking after the railings
And closing the rusty gate behind her.

SLUMBER

Why do you sleep with the bedroom door open?
You are both in your eighties and snore lightly.
There are photos from Ireland above your bedstead,
Downings and Donaghadee. Your marriage
Continues in slumber as I eavesdrop here.
You are like the babes in the wood, dear sister,
Elderly children a long, long way from home
In Mississauga where I am visiting you,
And you sleep with the bedroom door wide open.

PLACE-NAMES

I shall have lost my way
At last somewhere between
Traleckachoolia
And Carrignarooteen.

STARLINGS

Sitting up against a sea wall,
Eating fish and chips, we count
The starlings, a dozen or so
Swaggering opportunists
Unexpected on the shingle.
Shall we throw them leftovers,
Dear brother? Greasy fingers.
Spangled iridescences.
Is this Bangor or Ballyholme?
A blink and they attract thousands
And thousands more starlings, a shape-
Shifting bird-cloud, shitlegs
Sky-dancing. No collisions.
Wherever you are, Peter,
Can you spot on your radar
Angels? They're starlings really,
Heavenly riffraff flocking
Before they flap down to roost.

BIRD-WATCHING

I waken in dawn-light as tufted ducks
Settle among the residential swans
But fall asleep before counting them,
Then I open my eyes on lapwings —
Two dozen or more — circling the lake
And landing beside the Fairy Fort
Where I want my ashes wind-scattered.
I wouldn't mind dying now, I think,
Shutting at last my bird-watching eyes,
A starling-whoosh in my inner ear.

AGE

I have been writing about this townland
For fifty years, watching on their hummock
Autumn lady's tresses come and go and,
After a decade underground, return
In hundreds. I have counted the whoopers
And the jackdaws over Morrison's barn.
Too close on the duach to tractor tracks
The ringed plover's nest has kept me awake,
And the otter that drowned in an eel-trap.
Salvaging snail shells and magpie feathers
For fear of leaving particulars out,
I make little space for philosophising.
I walk ever more slowly to gate and stile.
Poetry is shrinking almost to its bones.

THE SISKIN'S EGG

Consider the siskin's egg,
Exquisitely dappled — spots
And dashes — lilac, pale
Reddish-brown, blood splashes
Across a greeny white —
Sunset at world's end — so,
Consider the siskin's egg.

THE WHIMBREL'S CALL

There are seven of them
Falling short of a trill —
Just — seven quick notes
From the long-beaked whimbrel
Night-flying overhead,
Whistling down the chimney
At nobody's address.

THE DIPPER'S RANGE

I walk beside the stream
Within the dipper's range:
Winter's only songbird,
Wild and melodious.

IMAGE

The last day of the year:
Greylag geese are flying
In regular formation
Along the shoreline, sky-shapes,
An image of poetry.

Notes & Acknowledgements

'The Magnifying Glass' was written for *For Fleur*, a festschrift compiled by Janet Wilson and Rod Edmond (New Zealand Studies Network and University of Northampton); 'Inlet' for *Kathleen Jamie: Essays and Poems on her Work*, edited by Rachel Falconer (Edinburgh University Press); 'Bookshops' for *Off the Shelf: A Celebration of Bookshops in Verse*, edited by Carol Ann Duffy (Picador).

'Riddle' was written for *The New Exeter Book of Riddles*, edited by Kevin Crossley-Holland and Lawrence Sail (Enitharmon); 'The Sonnets' for *On Shakespeare's Sonnets: A Poets' Celebration*, edited by Hannah Crawforth and Elizabeth Scott-Baumann (Bloomsbury).

'Snowdrops' was written for the inaugural Winchester Poetry Festival; and 'Storm' for *Keep it in the Ground*, an anthology of poetry on climate change, edited by Carol Ann Duffy for *The Guardian*.

Several of these poems have been published in two fine-art limited editions, with illustrations by Sarah Longley: *Sea Asters* and *The Dipper's Range* (Andrew J. Moorhouse, Fine Press Poetry); and in a chapbook, *Twelve Poems* (Clutag Press).

'The Troubles' was inspired by John Wilson Foster, one of Ireland's most distinguished public intellectuals. The answer to 'Riddle' is *gorse, whin, furze*.

Some of these poems have appeared previously in *Agenda*, *Archipelago*, *Freckle*, *The Guardian*, *The Irish Times*, the *London Review of Books*, *The New Yorker*, *Ploughshares*, *Poetry London*, *The Poetry Review*, *Poetry Ireland Review*, *Southword*, *Yellow Nib*; and on RTE and BBC.

Three oft-repeated glosses: *townland* is a rural term for an area of land that varies from a few acres to thousands; *duach* is a sandy plain behind dunes that affords some grazing; *lazybeds* are disused potato drills.

Look at all the colours
You could paint the world
Maisie Rendall says